Authenticity in Christopher Isherwood's Autobiographical Works. A Comparative Analysis

Julia Reuter

Bibliographic information published by the German National Library:

The German National Library lists this publication in the National Bibliography; detailed bibliographic data are available on the Internet at http://dnb.dnb.de.

ISBN: 9783346965523
This book is also available as an ebook.

© GRIN Publishing GmbH
Trappentreustraße 1
80339 München

Print and binding: Books on Demand GmbH, Norderstedt, Germany
Printed on acid-free paper from responsible sources.

The present work has been carefully prepared. Nevertheless, authors and publishers do not incur liability for the correctness of information, notes, links and advice as well as any printing errors.

GRIN web shop: https://www.grin.com/document/1416290

Humboldt Universität zu Berlin

Centre for British Studies

The Question of Authenticity in Christopher Isherwood's Autobiographical Writings

Master Thesis

28 February 2011

Julia Reuter

TABLE OF CONTENTS

Mr Norris had two front doors to his flat. They stood side by side. Both had little round peep-holes in the centre panel and brightly polished knobs and brass nameplates. On the left-hand plate was engraved: *Arthur Norris. Private.* And on the right hand: *Arthur Norris. Export and Import.* [...] I noticed immediately I was inside, [that] the Private side of the entrance hall was divided from the Export side only by a thick hanging curtain.

From *Mr Norris Changes Trains* by Christopher Isherwood

1. Autobiographical Glimpses

According to one of his biographers, Christopher Isherwood's "principal characteristic, both in his life and his work, was an apparent candour; he was also a professional charmer" (Parker 2004: n.p.). Isherwood's works have been rediscovered thanks to Tom Ford's film adaptation of *A Single Man*, released in 2009, and to the recent publication of a second volume of diaries, *The Sixties* (2010).

All works of fiction are autobiographical to some extent, but this is especially true for Isherwood, who relied on his journals for inspiration for his books. Paul Piazza has described Isherwood's novels as "autobiographical glimpses [...] into a mirror" (Piazza 1978: 196). However, Isherwood also produced several works which permit the reader more than glimpses.

Scholarly discussion of the genre has come to the conclusion that autobiography can never portray an entirely authentic picture of the author's life. After all, life-writing is filtered twice, first through the subjectivity of perception, and then through the writing process, as the narrative imposes a logic and causality on the text that was never there in real life. This means that autobiography is not a record, but a creation, and in order to distract readers from this artificiality, writers usually simulate authenticity in their texts in some way.

This leads to the following questions: How does Isherwood construct authenticity in *his* autobiographical works? And how is the reader expected to respond?

In order to gain an understanding of this issue, some the most prevalent theories on autobiography will be applied to Isherwood's autobiographical novel *Lions and Shadows*[1] (1938), his family memoir *Kathleen and Frank* (1971), and his autobiography *Christopher and His Kind* (1976). These texts will be analysed according to specific criteria of authenticity, and compared with each other in order to determine the extent of Isherwood's "apparent candour" (Parker 2004: n.p.).

1.1. Brief Outline of Isherwood's Life[2]

Christopher William Bradshaw-Isherwood was born in Cheshire, England, on August 26, 1904. His father, Frank Isherwood, was descended from a family of the landed gentry, and his mother, Kathleen Machell Smith, was the daughter of a prosperous middle-class wine merchant.

---

[1] As will be demonstrated in chapter 2.1.1, *Lions and Shadows* is not entirely convincing as an autobiographical novel, but for simplicity's sake, it is referred to as such at this point.

[2] For a more comprehensive account, up to the year 1979, cf. Finney (1979). Peter Parker's acclaimed biography (2004) spans Isherwood's whole life.

Isherwood's father died in 1915 at the Battle of Ypres. While he was still in school, Isherwood met W.H. Auden and Edward Upward, who would remain two of his closest friends for the rest of his life. He started to read History at Cambridge University in 1923, but spent most of his time there creating a surrealist alternate universe called 'Mortmere' with Upward, and eventually left university without a degree in 1925. His first published novel, *All the Conspirators*, appeared in 1928, the year when Isherwood met Auden again and was introduced to Stephen Spender.

After a series of short-lived pursuits in England, Isherwood moved to Berlin in 1929, where he spent his days writing and teaching English. He used these experiences to write two of his most accomplished works, *Mr Norris Changes Trains* (1935) and *Goodbye to Berlin* (1939). He collaborated with Auden on three plays, and they went to China together, whereupon they published the travelogue *Journey to a War* (1939). *Lions and Shadows* appeared in 1938.

Isherwood and Auden immigrated to the USA in 1939, which was regarded as an inexcusable escape from the imminent Second World War by some members of the literary circle. While Auden stayed on in New York, Isherwood settled in California and converted to Vedantism. He went on to publish several spiritual works, some of them in collaboration with his guru, Swami Prabhavananda.

In 1946, Isherwood became a US citizen. He met Don Bachardy, who was going to be his partner for the rest of his life, in 1953. In the USA, he continued to publish novels, among them *A Single Man* (1964), and he regularly worked for the film industry in Hollywood. From 1959 onwards, he also taught at various southern Californian colleges.

Isherwood gained more international recognition when *Cabaret*, the musical adapted from the *Berlin Stories*, opened in New York in 1966. His fame increased further owing to the musical's 1973 film adaptation, starring Liza Minnelli. After his coming-out in *Kathleen and Frank* (1971) and the publication of *Christopher and His Kind* (1976), Isherwood became a symbol for the Californian gay-rights movement. He was diagnosed with prostate cancer in 1981 and died at home in Santa Monica on January 4, 1986.

1.2. A Theory of Autobiography

This chapter lists some of the leading theories on autobiography, focusing on those which are most valuable for the purpose of this thesis.

The term 'autobiography' literally means that a person's life story is written down by that person themselves, but scholarly discussion of the genre has been trying to produce a more

2

2. Authenticity in Isherwood's Works

The criteria established above manifest themselves in one way or another in all three of the texts, but they are not equally pronounced in each of them. That is why the following chapters will focus on different criteria.

2.1. Lions and Shadows

Isherwood begins *Lions and Shadows*

> by saying what this book is not: it is not, in the ordinary journalistic sense of the word, an autobiography; it contains no 'revelations'; it is never 'indiscreet'; it is not even entirely 'true.' Its sub-title [sic] explains its purpose: to describe the first stages in a lifelong education—the education of a novelist. A young man living at a certain period in a certain European country, is subjected to a certain kind of environment, certain stimuli, certain influences. That the young man happens to be myself is only of secondary importance (Isherwood 1996: 5).

He promises that he will portray the education of a writer in the 1920s, and the reader is led to believe that Isherwood is a typical representative of this generation. He goes on to suggest that the book should be read "as a novel" (*ibid.*), implying that a fictionalised story is a more suitable way to achieve his goal and making it reminiscent of the traditional *künstlerroman*. In this type of novel, the protagonist is generally an artist, and the book follows their development from childhood to maturity (cf. Cuddon 1998: 446). A *künstlerroman* often includes a discussion of what it means to be an artist and of what inspires him or her. Prominent British examples of this genre are W. Somerset Maugham's *Of Human Bondage* (1915), James Joyce's *A Portrait of the Artist as a Young Man* (1916) and Virginia Woolf's *To the Lighthouse* (1927), all of which would probably have been known to an educated young man with an interest in literature like Isherwood.[3]

2.1.1. Fact or Fiction?

The notion that *Lions and Shadows* is based on the ideal of the *künstlerroman* is supported by the fact that its plot is quite similar to that of *A Portrait of the Artist as a Young Man*, depicting the protagonist's growth to maturity as well as his struggles against a restrictive social

---

[3] In fact, Isherwood mentions having read Maugham's and Woolf's works in *Christopher and His Kind* (cf. Isherwood 2001: 45; 113), but it is not entirely certain whether he did so before or after *Lions and Shadows* was published.

environment. Just like Joyce's Stephen Dedalus, Isherwood is shown to leave his homeland to make his way as an artist in mainland Europe.

However, a *künstlerroman* is typically written in the third person, while *Lions and Shadows* is narrated in the first person. Furthermore, in a *künstlerroman*, the author usually chooses an alter ego – Joyce disguises himself as 'Stephen Dedalus'. In *Lions and Shadows*, the protagonist is named Christopher Isherwood; even his full last name, Bradshaw-Isherwood, is mentioned (cf. Isherwood 1996: 126). This is very puzzling to the reader, as the shared name of author, narrator and protagonist is a feature of autobiography, as Lejeune has explained (cf. Lejeune 1989: 5).

Isherwood adds to the reader's confusion by claiming that *Lions and Shadows* is not an autobiography "in the ordinary journalistic sense of the word" (Isherwood 1996: 5). This implies that he does not intend the text to be a sensationalist portrayal of his life designed to shock the reader, and that he is writing for a 'serious' audience[4]. But is the reader supposed to infer that the book could be an autobiography 'in another sense'? Due to this vague note, they do not quite know what to expect.

This ambiguity can also be observed in Isherwood's construction and deconstruction of authenticity. On the one hand, he is very exact in his descriptions; for example, he paints a vivid picture of the school library (cf. *ibid.*: 10) as well as of his and Chalmers' rooms in Cambridge (cf. *ibid.*: 31-32; 61). The reader is informed of the exact amount of Isherwood's scholarship (cf. *ibid.*: 16; 29) and his income (cf. *ibid.*: 84; 123). He also quotes from poems written by his friends (cf. *ibid.*: 24-25; 43-44; 115-116) and from his own tripos papers (cf. *ibid.*: 80-82).

Another factor which suggests authenticity is Isherwood's use of the "private slang" (*ibid*: 40) he and Chalmers have developed; they use words like "blague" (*ibid.*: 20; 71) and "quisb" (*ibid.*: 49; 50; 62), and they refer to their sworn enemies as the "Poshocracy" (*ibid.*: 34), whom they frequently want to challenge with the words "*J'en appelle!*[5]" (*ibid.*: 45; 70; 96). The language in general is very conversational, with contractions and an unusual amount of dialogue. While the latter is also common in novels, in *Lions and Shadows*, it does not seem to fulfil the same function. In an almost documentary manner, Isherwood records speech patterns to heighten the text's authenticity – but this authenticity is merely staged because it only reveals the surface of conversations, not their contents.

---

[4] This is evidenced by the fact that he includes several French terms or passages (cf. Isherwood 1996: 87; 132), as well as an excerpt from the original Italian version of Dante's *Inferno* (cf. *ibid.*: 15), without providing translations.
[5] Isherwood and Chalmers translate this challenge (incorrectly) as "I'll see you!" (*ibid.*: 71)

There are no excerpts from his diary and only one from a letter (cf. *ibid.*: 103-106), which lessens the text's authenticity. While Isherwood's exactness in describing settings and speech patterns indicates that the text is an autobiography, the lack of original material from that period is a sign of fiction.

The text is written in the first person, with the exception of the references to 'Isherwood the Writer' (cf. below). However, the way in which Isherwood criticises himself does suggest that he can look back on his life with sufficient objectivity. There is a clear distinction between the narrated 'I' and the narrating 'I', with the latter having gained substantially in maturity and self-awareness. For example, when his fag loses his football boots, Isherwood admits that

> [t]here was an ugly, cold-blooded little ceremony, I used the words 'afraid' and 'sorry' with an hypocrisy worth of a grown-up man; then I let him wait three hours [...]; finally I sent for him, told him to bend over a chair and gave him the allowed maximum, three strokes. (*ibid.*: 27)

He mentions that "[Stephen Savage's] kindness was so touching and disarming that it sometimes made me quite irritable." (*ibid.*: 174) However, Isherwood's past and present selves are not presented as separate beings: "Most of what I wrote during those three days was dreadfully stupid [...]. When I read through all that nonsense now, I feel really ashamed." (*ibid.*: 81) At another point, he reflects that "[l]ooking back, I think that those first two University terms have been amongst the most enjoyable parts of my whole life" (*ibid.*: 45).

Most of the criticism levelled at Isherwood's former self is conveyed in a witty, ironic way. The majority of these passages refer to his early work as a writer, with Isherwood looking back on his failed attempts at publishing a novel from a perspective of success. The manuscript for an unpublished novel also called 'Lions and Shadows'[6] is referred to as a "curiosity for the psycho-analyst [sic]" (*ibid.*: 46). One publisher refuses the first draft of *All the Conspirators* (1928), then called 'Seascape with Figures', "saying that [his] work had 'a certain literary delicacy, but lacked sufficient punch'—a pretty damning verdict, when your story ends with a murder" (*ibid.*: 127). Isherwood makes fun of the pretentious plans he has for another novel, particularly the

> pseudo-technical terms invented for the occasion, such as 'fifth static area' or 'Tommy-roger Motif bridge-passage to Welsea.' I would wake up in the middle of the night to scribble emotionally in my note-book. 'The treatment must be nearly pure *Objective*. The Epic Myth. [...] Very slow-moving maddeningly deliberate genre-packed scenes. (*ibid.*)

---

[6] Isherwood describes this novel in detail. However, since it is not accessible to the public, it is impossible to confirm its existence. In order to distinguish it from the published *Lions and Shadows*, the title has been placed within single quotation marks. For the sake of consistency, the same has been done with any other – equally untraceable – unpublished works Isherwood mentions.

He also mocks the juvenile, dramatic image of the artist he had for a long time: "Isherwood the artist was an austere ascetic, cut off from the outside world, in voluntary exile, a recluse. […] He stood apart from and above 'The Test'— [but] was subjected, daily, hourly, to a 'Test' of his own: the self-imposed Test of his integrity as a writer." (*ibid*.: 60) He "imagined that 'being an artist' was a kind of neurotic alternative to being an ordinary human man" (*ibid*.: 76), a view which he contrasts with that of his mentor Cheuret, who "wasn't and didn't in the least feel himself to be 'exiled' from the world. My conception of 'Isherwood the Artist,' the lonely, excluded, monastic figure, was something he could never have understood." (*ibid*.: 91-92) It is his changing conception of the artist which shows that the protagonist is steadily maturing.

> "Isherwood the Artist" was still striking an attitude on his lonely rock. But his black Byronic exile's cloak failed to impress me any longer. I knew what was inside it now—just plain, cold, uninteresting funk. Funk of getting too deeply involved with other people, sex-funk, funk of the future. (*ibid*.: 187)

The fact that Isherwood's artist persona is referred to in the third person, although the book is written in the first person, suggests that they are two different beings, as tough Isherwood was not sure how to integrate this role into his identity. He grows bored of "Isherwood and his journal of lonely struggle and suffering" (*ibid*.: 60).

Isherwood frequently expresses a desire to be as truthful with himself as possible. "Now already I had to admit to myself that, as far as I was concerned, the entire ceremony had been altogether meaningless. If only I had been more honest with myself and avoided it, like Chalmers, from the very start!" (*ibid*.: 13) Isherwood and Chalmers invent a character named 'The Watcher in Spanish', who appears "at moments when our behaviour was particularly insincere" (*ibid*.: 33). The protagonist abandons his ideas for a novel because it is "a sham all through" (*ibid*.: 107). He also mocks other people whom he perceives to be insincere (cf. *ibid*. 149-151), while admiring Weston specifically because he is *not* a sham (cf. *ibid*.: 117-118).

The protagonist is increasingly aware of the fact that he is often merely playing a role: "at least seventy-five per cent of my 'personality' consisted in bad imitations of my various friends" (*ibid*.: 147). He performs with strangers (cf. *ibid*.: 153) and even with his own friends (cf. *ibid*.: 137; 177). One of the roles he plays is that of the outsider, which he claims he does not enjoy:

> Does anybody ever feel sincerely pleased at the prospect of remaining in permanent opposition, a social misfit, for the rest of his life? I knew, at any rate, that I myself didn't. I wanted— however much I might try to persuade myself, in moments of arrogance, to the contrary—to find some place, no matter how humble, in the scheme of society. Until I do that, I told myself, my writing will never be any good (*ibid*.: 152).

Indeed, this unhappiness with being an outsider does seem to be inextricably bound up with Isherwood's perception of the role of the writer:

> [B]eneath all my note-taking, my would-be scientific detachment, my hatred, my disgust, there was the old sense of exclusion, the familiar grudging envy. For, however I might sneer, these people *were* evidently enjoying themselves in their own mysterious fashion, and why was it so mysterious to me? [...] Why couldn't I—the would-be novelist, the professional observer—understand them? (*ibid.*)

It is when he finally admits to himself that he will not be able to go on studying medicine that Isherwood seems at his most sincere. He portrays it as a sort of dialogue with himself: "We know what you want, all right! The voice of your heart has told us already. You want to commit the unforgiveable sin, to shock Mummy and Daddy and Nanny, to smash the nursery clock" (*ibid.*: 188). He finally decides: "First of all I must leave England altogether—the break with the old life must be complete, this time—and [...] I'd go to Berlin." (*ibid.*) By 'quoting' this inner voice, Isherwood lends authenticity to the text. The desire to be truthful with himself suggests to the reader that he is also being honest with them.

Samuel Hynes believes that the protagonist is as much of a 'caricature' as any of the characters in *Lions and Shadows* (cf. Hynes 1976: 324). If this were the case, it would certainly argue for the text being a novel. However, examined in the context of Isherwood's later autobiographical writing, one can see that – although several important pieces of information are missing – the protagonist is still very much Isherwood himself.

The distance between narrator and protagonist, as well as the narrator's self-critical attitude, could indicate that *Lions and Shadows* is an autobiography, written by a more mature and thus objective author. On the other hand, it could also be a sign that the book is a *künstlerroman*, of which the author's objectivity is a necessary feature, as they are presumably not writing about themselves. In any case, this criterion clearly serves to heighten the text's authenticity.

However, Isherwood deconstructs this authenticity by admitting that the memory he has to rely on is full of gaps, for instance in the following lines: "Of the examination itself I remember very little" (Isherwood 1996: 16) and "I forget what he looked like." (*ibid.*: 167) Although Isherwood seems especially sincere in these passages, the reader is reminded of the fact that the text is not fully authentic. When Isherwood claims that he is "paraphrasing Barnard's own words, from a letter that Weston once showed [him]" (*ibid.*: 184), it might seem at first that, since he is quoting the expert, his argument is more authentic. But the fact remains that he was shown this letter only once, so how could he possibly be able to quote from it at all?

Indeed, in some places, it seems as though Isherwood were covering up the fallibility of his memory: "I can hear him now" (*ibid.*: 7) or "I see him striding towards me" (*ibid.*: 116). He includes a number of such audiovisual memories (cf. *ibid.*: 112; 113; 138). This suggests that some recollections are stronger than others, presumably those which concern friends. For example, Isherwood notes that "thinking about Stephen as he was in those days, I like specially to remember one incident" (*ibid.*: 174). Elsewhere, he claims that "I remember [Weston] chiefly for his naughtiness" (*ibid.*: 112). He is drawing the reader's attention to the fact that memory is selective, that we focus on certain events and tend to forget others.

On the other hand, Isherwood records entire conversations (cf. *ibid.*: 14; 19; 86-87) and passages from a novel that a schoolmate is writing (cf. *ibid.*: 11). This is before he starts keeping a journal (cf. *ibid.*: 59), so how could he possibly remember things in such detail? Due to these factors *Lions and Shadows* could be interpreted as a novel. In fact, Isherwood admits at one point that it "would be easy to dramatize my emotions on this portentous but unexciting journey—easy, because I have forgotten altogether what they were" (*ibid.*: 191). He is reminding the reader that if you forget a piece of information, you can just as easily invent another. He also calls attention to the fact that he has the power to censor his material: "The rest, unfortunately, is not printable" (*ibid.*: 44). "Bradshaw-Isherwood, my ponderous double-barrelled name, hitherto so carefully ignored in these pages" (*ibid.*: 126). Again, these acknowledgments of the genre's limitations suggest that *Lions and Shadows* is a novel, of which gaps in the narrative are a common feature. Alternatively, it could also be construed as an autobiography, with Isherwood demonstrating his sincerity by reminding the reader of the shortcomings of the autobiographical form. This confusion is illustrated by a very illuminating passage in which the protagonist is talking to a shop girl. She asks him questions about his life and he replies truthfully that he is a sort of schoolmaster, who teaches Latin, among other things, and that he is writing a novel. But he tells it to her in such a way that she thinks he is joking (cf. *ibid.*: 147-148). This shows that if one speaks of something in a certain way, such as by altering one's tone or by wording things differently, even the truth can seem unlikely, which undermines the dichotomy of fact and fiction.

Since *Lions and Shadows* focuses on Isherwood's work as a writer, it should not be surprising that there are many references to his novels, published and unpublished. What is unusual, however, is the amount of detail in which these works are described. Isherwood documents the themes and plot of his unpublished first novel 'Lions and Shadows' (cf. *ibid.*: 45-49), his ideas for 'Christopher Garland' (cf. *ibid.*: 75-76), and for 'The North-West Passage' (cf. *ibid.*: 129-

131), as well as the plot of what will eventually be published as *The Memorial* (cf. *ibid.*: 182-183).

Both the storylines and the themes are reminiscent of Isherwood's life as laid out in *Lions and Shadows*. Fact and fiction generally seem to be very closely interwoven in his work. For example, he reveals his plans to write "an immense novel: nothing less ambitious than a survey of the post-war generation. [...] All my friends were to appear: Chalmers, Philip, Eric, Weston, the Cheurets—and, of course, myself." (*ibid.*: 127) When he mentions the landlady he will be living with in Berlin later on in his life, he calls her "Frl Schroeder" (*ibid.*: 172), which is the fictitious name Isherwood uses in *Goodbye to Berlin*. Regarding his friend Bill's warning not to move to Berlin, he concedes that "looking back, I can see clearly what he did mean: and certainly, in a sense, he was right. I must refer my readers, here, to my novel, *Mr. Norris Changes Trains!*" (*ibid.*: 189) Fiction is portrayed as equally suitable for the search for authenticity as autobiography.

Another work of fiction which Isherwood extensively comments on are the stories set in the imaginary village of 'Mortmere' which he and Chalmers have conceived (cf. *ibid.*: 62-70; 100-103). These passages not only serve to illustrate the young Isherwood's view of the world, but they are also presented as invaluable to his education as a writer. The work he does with Chalmers has clearly strengthened his ability to structure plots and to invent absorbing characters.

Although Isherwood subverts the contrast between reality and fiction, as an author, he really did publish novels entitled *All the Conspirators* and *The Memorial*, a fact that the reader can easily confirm. This suggests that the text is an autobiography.

Lions and Shadows is divided into seven chapters, each of which focuses on a different setting or time period. Furthermore, each chapter concentrates on one of Isherwood's friends or mentors, the person who especially helps or influences him at this point in his life. For example, the first chapter recounts his last few years at public school and shows how his history teacher, Mr. Holmes, inspires him. This structure limits the text's authenticity and indicates that it is a novel; after all, life could hardly be divided into such clear-cut episodes.

It is evident that *Lions and Shadows* is exceedingly ambiguous in its messages. While some criteria clearly point to the text being either an autobiography or a novel, most can be interpreted as indicators of both. Thus, the text can be ascribed to neither of these categories. Furthermore, it is important to keep in mind that fiction can easily imitate any attributes of the autobiographical genre. "Narrative 'truth' is judged by its verisimilitude rather than its verifiability" (Bruner 1991: 13), a fact that Isherwood might well have been conscious of, considering that he placed the word 'true' within quotation marks in the note to the reader (cf. Isherwood 1996: 5). The only sign which Lejeune would regard as proof that a text is an autobiography is the identical name of author, narrator and protagonist. However, fiction could mimic even this feature.

2.1.2. Gaps in the Narrative

Why would Isherwood present this text as a novel in the first place? According to John Mullan, "autobiography must explain; a novel can make a narrative out of gaps. Fiction artfully omits." (Mullan 2007: n.p.) Isherwood manipulates the reader's literary response by encouraging them to read fictionally and to ignore any gaps that might manifest themselves. While an autobiography is expected to include details on the subject's social environment, a novel can neglect these.

And indeed, *Lions and Shadows* does not contain a lot of material which could be construed as very private. There are several references to the protagonist's sexuality, but these are all rather vague. It is important to remember that homosexual acts were illegal in Great Britain until the Sexual Offences Act 1967. On the other hand, considering that Isherwood is presenting the text as a novel, he could be more open, as he is presumably writing about the actions of other people.

Whenever the topic of Isherwood's sexuality is addressed, the reader suspects that the narrator is holding back: "Needless to say, Chalmers and myself were both virgins, in every possible meaning of the word." (Isherwood 1996: 22) Isherwood explains that Chalmers "was beginning to find Cambridge absolutely intolerable. [...] He was sexually unsatisfied and lonely: he wanted a woman with whom he could fall in love and go to bed" (*ibid.*: 73-74). "I was unhappy, too; but less consciously so because, being in a much more complex psychological mess than Chalmers himself, I had evolved a fairly efficient system of censorships and compensations." (*ibid.*: 74) The reader gets the impression that Isherwood is confessing something vital about himself, but what exactly that is remains unclear. Recounting the basic plot of his unpublished novel 'Lions and Shadows', he describes "the central figure, the dream I, [as] an austere young prefect, [...] grimly repressing his own romantic feelings towards a younger boy, and finally triumphing over all his obstacles, passing the test, emerging—a Man. Need I confess any more?" (*ibid.*: 48) This could be taken as a hint that the narrator himself is homosexual, an idea that is strengthened by the following passage; describing his memories of the 1926 General Strike, Isherwood says that "'war' was in the air: one heard it in the boisterous defiant laughter of the amateur bus drivers, one glimpsed it in the alert sexual glances of the women." (*ibid.*: 110) Considering the fact that Isherwood seems to equate a woman's sexuality with 'war', the next statement should not come as a surprise: "the majority of the men were secretly embarrassed at finding themselves practically naked in the presence of a lot of semi-naked and (presumably to them) attractive girls." (*ibid.*: 151) Isherwood "found that [he] was particularly good at cuddling; especially after three or four 'dog's noses' (gin and beer) at the pub. Indeed, my very inhibitions made me extremely daring—up to a point." (*ibid.*: 155) He contrasts his attitude with that of his friend Tim, "who really meant business" (*ibid.*) – implying that he himself does not. Isherwood truly seems to go as far as possible without implicating himself in then illegal acts.

The narrator is astounded at Weston's relaxed attitude to sex:

> I compared him with Chalmers. When Chalmers and I were together there were, and had always been, certain reticences between us: parts of our lives were common ground, other parts were not—and these, by mutual consent, we respected and left alone. (*ibid.*: 120)

Isherwood does not elaborate on these 'reticences'. But unlike Chalmers, "Weston left nothing alone and respected nothing: he intruded everywhere; upon my old-maidish tidyness [sic], my intimate little fads, my private ailments, my most secret sexual fears." (*ibid.*)

> Weston's own attitude to sex, in its simplicity and utter lack of inhibition, fairly took my breath away. He was no Don Juan: he didn't run round hunting for his pleasures. But he took what came to him with a matter-of-factness and an appetite as hearty as that which he showed when sitting down to dinner. (*ibid.*: 121)

Although the narrator certainly hints at the fact that the protagonist is homosexual, he never explicitly says so. The reader suspects that a vital piece of information is missing, which limits the text's authenticity.

Incomplete though the information on Isherwood's sexuality may be, another personal topic, his family, is hardly mentioned at all. An exceedingly blurry presence, there are only a few references to "my relatives" (*ibid.*: 87) or "my family" (*ibid.*: 121; 122; 166; 178); the only instance in which specific people are mentioned is this passage: "You want to commit the unforgiveable sin, to shock Mummy and Daddy and Nanny, to smash the nursery clock, to be a really naughty little boy." (*ibid.*: 188) It is clear that the influence of the narrator's family is far greater than he is letting on:

> One always has to go back, I thought, at the end of these little escapades. You may give your familiar everyday self the slip easily enough; for several hours, your absence won't be noticed, and if your car is fast and you can keep on the run you may even escape for a whole week. But, sooner or later, you will come to a halt; sooner or later, that dreary governess, that gloomy male nurse will catch you up; will arrive, on the slow train, to fetch you back to your nursery prison of minor obligations, duties, habits, ties. (*ibid.*: 165-66)

Isherwood seems to contrast his identity within his family, his 'familiar everyday self', with his self as a writer. He feels trapped: "It was hopeless. As long as I remained at home, I could never expect to escape from my familiar tiresome, despicable self." (*ibid.*: 122)

A statement that can only be decoded with the help of *Kathleen and Frank* is the following:

> I had arrived at my public school thoroughly sick of masters and mistresses, having been emotionally messed about by them at my preparatory school, where the war years had given full licence to every sort of dishonest cant about loyalty, selfishness, patriotism, playing the game and dishonouring the dead. Now I wanted to be left alone. (*ibid.*: 9)

After reading his family memoir, the reader knows that Isherwood is talking about the fact that his father died at Ypres in 1915, and that, as a young boy, he was constantly told he must live up to his father's memory. In *Lions and Shadows*, however, this passage remains rather unclear. Although this obscurity hints at the existence of an authentic back region, the reader is not permitted to see beyond the front region.

War is another subject that remains full of gaps. When Isherwood is having a conversation with a veteran named Lester, it seems that only Lester is talking, while Isherwood hardly reveals his own feelings:

> He never suspected, I think, how violently his quietly told horribly matter-of-fact anecdotes affected me. [...] Always, as I listened I asked myself the same question; always I tried to picture myself in his place. But here, as ever, the censorship, in blind panic, intervened, blacking out the image. (*ibid.*: 157)

Although Isherwood does not say so, he is probably also imagining his father on the battlefield. He claims that

> we young writers of the middle 'twenties were all suffering, more or less subconsciously, from a feeling of shame that we hadn't been old enough to take part in the European war. The shame, I have said, was subconscious: in my case, at any rate, it was suppressed by the strictest possible censorship. (*ibid.*: 46)

Isherwood does not clarify why he alone is in this particular situation, why he censors himself to this extent. "Like most of my generation, I was obsessed by a complex of terrors and longings connected with the idea 'War.' 'War,' in this purely neurotic sense, meant The Test. The Test of your courage, of your maturity, of your sexual prowess: 'Are you really a Man?'" (*ibid.*) However, for Isherwood the Test does not exist for the 'Truly Strong Man':

> calm, balanced, aware of his strength, […] it is not necessary for him to try and prove to himself that he is not afraid […]. In other words, the Test exists only for the Truly Weak Man: no matter whether he passes it or whether he fails, he cannot alter his essential nature. (*ibid.*: 128)

According to Hynes, "the Truly Weak Man is a central 'thirties character, and the Test is his typical situation" (Hynes 1976: 127). Similar personas can be found in Auden's and Spender's oeuvre. However, both of these writers were heavily influenced by Isherwood in their early works. In the context of *Lions and Shadows*, these passages are somewhat perplexing, as the reader does not fully understand the source of the protagonist's feelings.

As mentioned above, it is entirely possible for fiction to leave gaps in the narrative. However, due to these obscure passages, the protagonist does not seem like a fully comprehensible, three-dimensional character – something that should be avoided in a novel. The text's authenticity is limited by the fact that Isherwood does *not* address any private issues or break any taboos.

2.1.3. Promises Kept?

Isherwood has told the reader that *Lions and Shadows* is designed to illustrate the education of a novelist in the 1920s, suggesting that the events portrayed could have happened to any other novelist of that generation. According to Jonathan Bolton, the authors of most British autobiographies published between 1938 and 1950 claim to speak for an entire generation (cf. Bolton 2006: 156; 157). Admittedly, the 'stimuli' and the 'environment' young men were "subjected to" (Isherwood 1996: 5) were shared by members of the upper and upper-middle class: a privileged upbringing and an education at public school, then Cambridge or Oxford. However, Isherwood does not only address his 'official' education, i.e. the education he received at school and at Cambridge, but, more importantly, he demonstrates how his friends and mentors inspired him.

The reader is therefore constantly aware of the fact that the 'young man' portrayed in the novel 'happens to be' Isherwood himself. Also, most of the pseudonyms employed by the author to prevent 'hurt feelings' are not very convincing. For example, his friend 'Hugh Weston' can quite easily be decoded as the poet Wystan Hugh Auden, and 'Stephen Savage' is clearly Stephen Spender.[7] As they were public figures and part of the 'Auden Group', most of Isherwood's readership would have been familiar with their names.

Due to the vagueness of Isherwood's references to his family and sexuality, the reader constantly suspects that Isherwood is holding back important facts about himself. In the case of his sexuality, this is certainly understandable, considering the legal restrictions at the time. But the text is supposed to record the education of Isherwood as a writer, and these issues are certain to have played a role in this development. In *A Portrait of the Artist as a Young Man*, the protagonist's family and sexuality are very important factors in shaping his character. But a prerequisite of being representative is being 'normal'. Perhaps Isherwood left these gaps in the narrative precisely *because* they would have exposed him as 'not normal'. And by hinting at the existence of a back region, he is retaining his individuality while also fitting himself into a broader context.

2.2. Kathleen and Frank

Kathleen and Frank can be described as a family memoir, although Isherwood never explicitly establishes it as such. According to Francis R. Hart, "a memoir is the personal record of historic events and persons" (Hart 1970: 510). Instead of spanning the author's whole life, like most autobiographies do, it "seeks to articulate or repossess the historicity of the self" (*ibid.*: 491), which can clearly be observed in *Kathleen and Frank*.

First of all, the narrator tries to convince the reader that the text is worth reading. After all, these are regular Victorian[8] people, so why should their lives be relevant to the reader at all?

> Kathleen was careful to be exact about names, dates and even times of day, but she did much more than record happenings, she tried to evoke places and atmospheres, she wrote with a strong consciousness of personal and national drama, of herself and the England she was living in. She saw her own life as History (Isherwood 1971: 1-2).

And indeed, the narrator takes care to invoke an historic atmosphere, including those passages in Kathleen's diary which refer to late-Victorian life, its customs and its etiquettes, but also to political events, such as Queen Victoria's Diamond Jubilee (cf. *ibid.*: 28) and death (cf. *ibid.*:

[7] This is confirmed by reviews published in 1938 (cf. Grigson 1938: 19). Although the book did receive a fair amount of attention by critics, its sales figures were rather low. Random House Library Manager Jean Rose reports that by 1 October 1942, the book had sold only 2234 times (cf. Rose 2011: n.p.). However, these figures were without a doubt affected by the war.

[8] Although only a third of the book portrays Victorian times, both Kathleen and Frank had passed their thirtieth year by the time of Queen Victoria's death in 1901. Thus, they were essentially Victorian people, whose values and beliefs were shaped by that age (cf. Isherwood 1971: 345).

108), and the coronation as well as death of Edward VII (cf. *ibid.*: 152; 249). The narrator promises that Kathleen and Frank's history is authentic and "worth retelling" (*ibid.*: 208), and the reader is encouraged to see their lives as history, too.

The connection between Christopher, Kathleen and Frank is clarified immediately:

> Christopher, her elder son, revolted early and passionately against the cult of the Past. [H]e learnt to hate and fear the Past because it threatened to swallow his future. [...] Nevertheless, Christopher grew up to become a recorder, too, and so, willy-nilly, a celebrant of the Past; he began to keep a diary and to write autobiographical novels. (*ibid.*: 2)

In this way, a parallel between Christopher and his parents is drawn, but at first glance, the book still appears to focus on Kathleen and Frank, as the title suggests. It begins with Kathleen's first diary entry and ends with her death. A large proportion of the text consists of excerpts from her diaries and from letters written to her by Frank. These are structured in a strictly chronological manner. Around them darts the narrator's commentary, commencing at the present day, and then going back and forth in time. These observations are clearly marked as Isherwood's and are thus easily distinguishable from the 'original' material, which is a claim for the text's authenticity.[9] The narrator's role is comparable to that of an interpreter, and it is he who has the power to select material and to direct the reader's eye to where he wants it to be. As he is imposing an ex-post interpretation on the events, he can point out specific things he knows proved to be important in hindsight.

2.2.1. The Relevance of Kathleen's and Frank's Lives

In order to construct authenticity, the narrator takes care to be as specific as possible with regard to the protagonists' surroundings. There are entire chapters detailing Frank's every move during the Second Boer War (cf. *ibid.*: 56-73; 114-139) and the First World War (cf. *ibid.*: 290-328). An extensive passage recounts the history of the Bradshaw family (cf. *ibid.*: 207-217), mostly focusing on John Bradshaw, the man who was chosen as Lord President of the High Court which sentenced Charles I to death.

However, Isherwood bases most of his account on Kathleen's diary and Frank's letters. The sources do not appear to have been altered; for example, Isherwood has retained abbreviations (cf. *ibid.*: 103; 155; 195). Although editing the material might have improved its readability, the fact that it has (presumably) been left unchanged heightens its authenticity.

---

[9] In the original British edition, the excerpts from letters and diaries are printed in a smaller font, suggesting that the narrator's commentary is more important. In some subsequent editions, the commentary has been italicised, ostensibly turning the order of importance around.

The narrator appears to have the mindset of an historian, which is not surprising, given that Isherwood himself read History:

> Kathleen's 1914 diary has the morbid fascination of a document which records, without the dishonesty of hindsight, the day-to-day approach to a catastrophe by an utterly unsuspecting victim. Meanwhile, as so often happens, this victim expects and fears a different catastrophe – civil war in Ulster – which isn't going to take place. (*ibid.*: 279)

Having Kathleen, a fairly ordinary citizen, comment on political developments such as the run-up to the Great War and the Home Rule Crisis presents a degree of authenticity that would not exist if Isherwood had only included official documents. Rather, by presenting documents, newspaper clippings (cf. *ibid.*: 307-308; 318) as well as comments on the public's reaction to these events, Isherwood is seemingly showing the reader a balanced view on history. The fact that Kathleen lacks "the dishonesty of hindsight" (*ibid.*: 279) further supports the claim of authenticity. However, at the same time, the narrator criticises her choice in newspapers (cf. *ibid.*: 288), suggesting that he is the one who is portraying a more accurate version of the events.

Kathleen and Frank are depicted as fairly regular Victorian people. For example, Isherwood frequently expresses his bafflement at the etiquettes and particularities of this time (cf. *ibid.*: 30; 31; 173). The fact that Kathleen was almost nine months older than Frank was constantly remarked upon by his father (cf. *ibid.*: 87). Kathleen and Frank were engaged for almost two years before it was even announced in the press, due to her father's initial rejection of Frank as a suitable husband for her. Isherwood explains some of the idiosyncrasies of the upper class:

> In 1909, when Nanny was away on holiday and Christopher was nearing his fifth birthday, Kathleen records that she helped him wash and dress himself *for the first time*. [...] During the Age of Nannies such a state of affairs wasn't unusual in upper-class homes, [Kathleen] had to be a wife and daughter first, a mother second. [...] Nevertheless, Kathleen's frequent absences had their effect; particularly on [Christopher's brother,] Richard. He recalls that, when he was four years old, Kathleen was a 'semi-stranger of whom I was a bit in awe. (*ibid.*: 197-198)

According to the narrator, Kathleen found herself "caught in a generation-gap. On one side of her is the generation of the Martyr-Wife; on the other, the generation of the New Woman." (*ibid.*: 38) This conflict is evidenced by some of her opinions. After Christopher birth, "Mr Isherwood said I had done my duty and done it well!! To which I quite agreed." (*ibid.*: 195) Her ironic tone reveals that she did hold some of the views of the New Woman, but she was not progressive enough to join the Suffragettes (cf. *ibid.*: 242).

Isherwood not only illustrates his parents' relevance with regard to English history, but also their influence on his own development. He continually tries to establish parallels between himself and his parents. Frank Isherwood was an enthusiastic painter (cf. *ibid.*: 190; 203) and an amateur actor (cf. *ibid.*: 190). Although Kathleen disliked both the theatre (cf. *ibid.*: 89) and any literature that was not "soothingly written" (*ibid.*: 19), she was an accomplished watercolourist and a writer, describing herself as "a slave to [her] diary" (*ibid.*: 1). Furthermore, she and her mother published a book on historic walks in London, entitled *Our Rambles in Old London* (cf. *ibid.*: 15). Frank took it upon himself to teach his son literature (cf. *ibid.*: 252) and started "publishing a paper called the 'The Toy-Draw [sic] Times' every morning, illustrated!" (*ibid.*: 251-252) Just as Kathleen had an aversion to the German language, Christopher disliked learning French. Observing that "[a]ctually both of them were rebelling against the 'in' language of their generation" (*ibid.*: 4), Isherwood establishes a connection between himself and his mother. He also talks about his parents' religious beliefs:

> [T]o Kathleen, Christianity meant traditional worship publicly shared and church-going was its essential expression. [Frank] was temperamentally attracted to the philosophy of Hinduism and Buddhism [...] because it taught a private religion of self-effort, self-knowledge and solitary meditation. Christopher and Richard were later to follow Frank in this. Both grew up, largely because of their experiences of public religion at school, with a horror of The Church. (*ibid.*: 190)

It is obvious that Isherwood has chosen these passages to point out the similarities and differences between himself and his parents. However, this has the effect that Christopher is never fully in the shadows, but is mentioned throughout the text, even when he is not yet born.

It is in the afterword that Isherwood makes peace with his heritage. After having found two of the letters his father sent to his mother during the First World War, he was astonished to read the following words: "I don't think it matters very much what Christopher learns as long as he remains himself and keeps his individuality and develops on his own lines" (*ibid.*: 318). "The whole point of sending him to school was to flatten him out, so to speak, and to make him like other boys and, when all is said and done, I don't know that it is at all desirable or necessary, and I for one would much rather have him as he is." (*ibid.*: 321) As a young boy, he twisted his father's words according to his own needs:

> [H]e began to see their enormous value to himself, as a statement of Frank's last wishes and a speech for his defence [...]. Christopher interpreted this freely as '*Don't* follow in my footsteps! [...] Be anything except the son The Others tell you you ought to be. I *should* be ashamed of that kind of son. I want an Anti-Son. I want him to horrify The Others and disgrace my name in their eyes. I shall look on and applaud!' (*ibid.*: 359)

He did this in response to his teachers' claims that as a "Sacred Orphan" (*ibid.*: 356), he must try to live up to his father's ideal at all times. The reader is reminded of the passage in *Lions and Shadows* in which Isherwood remarks that the teachers at his preparatory school have been given "full licence to every sort of dishonest cant about loyalty, selfishness, patriotism, playing the game, and dishonouring the dead" (Isherwood 1996: 9). In light of the account laid out in *Kathleen and Frank*, this passage suddenly makes a lot more sense. Other comments bear a strong resemblance to those in *Lions and Shadows* which refer to 'The Test':

> The Anti-Heroic Hero always appears in uniform because this is his disguise; he isn't really a soldier. He is an artist who has renounced his painting, music and writing in order to dedicate his life to an anti-military masquerade. He lives this masquerade right through, day by day to the end, and crowns his performance by actually getting himself killed in battle. By thus fooling everybody (except Christopher) into believing he is the Hero-Father, he demonstrates the absurdity of the military mystique and its solemn cult of War and Death. (Isherwood 1971: 358)

Isherwood's idea of the 'Truly Strong Man' can clearly be traced back to these thoughts about his father, but in *Lions and Shadows*, the reader is kept unaware of this, as Frank's early death during wartime is not mentioned.

Although he idolises Frank, the narrator is also conscious of the fact that, while he missed a fatherly presence in his life, his relationship with his father might not have been very positive, had he survived:

> He might have tried hard to understand Christopher as a young man of the Freudian Twenties, but how could he possibly have succeeded, with all his prejudices, his snobbery, his 'Early English' attitudes? At best they might have agreed to differ like gentlemen, after Christopher had wasted years of precious youth-time breaking the dreadful news slowly to Frank about boy-love – then later about marxism [sic], and finally pacifism. It was more likely that Frank would have forgotten he had ever wanted Christopher to 'develop on his own lines'; that he would have ended by disowning this Anti-Son. (*ibid.*: 360)

The narrator not only makes peace with his father, but also with his "Holy Widow-Mother" (*ibid.*: 359), who played an entirely different role in his life. Christopher frequently clashed with Kathleen, a "devotee of the Past" (*ibid.*: 1; cf. *ibid.*: 218; 240; 352). She was a very overbearing figure, and "[a]t one time or another he was to blame Kathleen for almost all of her decisions affecting his future" (*ibid.*: 194). "But Christopher did need Kathleen" (*ibid.*: 360), "he would have lost the counter-force which gave him strength. It was Kathleen, more than anybody else, who saved him from becoming a mother's boy, a churchgoer, an academic, a conservative, a patriot and a respectable citizen." (*ibid.*: 361) "Kathleen, he knew, felt their quarrels deeply and grieved over them in private. Yet he didn't feel guilty. He could see that they gave her strength as well as himself." (*ibid.*: 362) The narrator shows his maturity by accepting that his parents have made him who he is.

2.2.2. Chiefly about Christopher?

Although it supposedly focuses on Kathleen and Frank, the previous chapter shows that the narrator is a strong presence in the book as well. In fact, Isherwood used *Kathleen and Frank* as a sort of public coming-out. A number of passages hint at the fact that his uncle Henry was homosexual (cf. *ibid.*: 81; 161; 188), and, finally, there is an (almost) explicit admission of Christopher's own homosexuality:

> As Heathcliff he imagined himself standing all night in a storm outside Catherine Linton's window; Catherine being for the moment a blond boy with a charming grin and long legs, who played hockey. (*ibid.*: 179-180)

Kathleen's attitude towards her son's sexuality is contrasted with that of his nanny's: he "loved Nanny dearly. He bullied her and ordered her around but rewarded her by telling her his secrets. [...] He let her see him coming home drunk at night [...]. He even made it obvious which of his friends he was going to bed with" (*ibid.*: 198). He could be "shameless and at ease" (*ibid.*) with her. The fact that Isherwood is sharing these private memories with the reader suggests that he can be just as 'at ease' with them. However, these frank admissions cause Christopher to step out of the shadows as a narrator, and the proportion of commentary compared to that of documentary material becomes greater.

Several of Isherwood's revelations would certainly have been quite shocking to a 1971 audience. "Wrestling soon became a conscious sex-pleasure. He found boxing sexy too, even though he usually got knocked about." (*ibid.*: 286) Some of his confessions have decidedly incestuous overtones:

> As a teacher, Frank was fairly patient. But sometimes he would fly into rages with Christopher and shake him till his teeth rattled. Christopher may have been frightened a little, but this too is a sensual memory for him: his surrender to the exciting strength of the big angry man. (*ibid.*: 252)

> Henry referred to Christopher as 'my favourite nephew' and recommended his books to his friends. Their bond wasn't literature, however, but the discovery that they had similar sexual tastes. When they dined together at Henry's flat, they giggled like age-mates over Henry's adventures with guardsmen and Christopher's encounters in the boy-bars of Berlin. [...] At the end of the evening he would be drunk and so would Henry – with the result that Christopher would get a goodnight kiss which was too warm and searching for any nephew, even one's favourite.[10] (*ibid.*: 349-350)

---

[10] Interestingly, Isherwood was to describe these evenings with his uncle in more or less the exact same words during an interview in 1973: "At the end of the evening, I would get a kiss from him which was rather too warm and searching for any nephew, even one's favorite." (Berg 2001: 108) It seems almost as though putting his thoughts on paper had fixed them in his mind in a certain way, which speaks for the power of writing.

Frank himself exercised every morning in his dressing room, naked except for his underpants. He let Christopher come in and watch him. Christopher can remember taking a pleasure which was definitely erotic in the sight of his Father's muscles tensing and bulging within his well-knit body. [sic] and in the virile smell of his sweat. But when Christopher began to masturbate (which he did while at Frimley) his fantasies weren't about Frank He imagined himself lying wounded on a battlefield with his clothes partly torn off him, being tended by a woman; Kathleen, no doubt, in disguise. (*ibid.* 252)

This sounds quite Freudian, a suspicion which is confirmed later:

After he had grown up, one of his friends assured him that his fear [of snakes] was nothing but a repressed longing to submit to anal intercourse. 'You want it to crawl into your arse.' They were all amateur Freudians in those days (*ibid.*: 254).

Some of these comments appear rather gratuitous, but there are also several passages which analyse his sexual development in a more serious manner. While his father was stationed in Limerick, Christopher was transferred to another class, one which had more boys in it than the previous one.

This change of schools was, of course, made in the hope that Christopher would become more masculine in male society. Kathleen took it for granted that his growing interest in girls was due to a girlishness in himself and nothing more. But perhaps she was wrong. Perhaps Christopher was actually exhibiting slight heterosexual tendencies which could have been strengthened and confirmed, if he had been sent to a co-educational school in his teens. [...] Well, thank goodness for St. Edmund's School and Repton, if they did indeed have anything to do with tipping the balance in the opposite direction. Despite the humiliations of living under a heterosexual dictatorship and the fury he has often felt against it, Christopher has never regretted being as he is. (*ibid.*: 272-273)

The text is written in the third person, and Isherwood appears as 'Christopher', even in his present self (cf. *ibid.*: 218). This affords him the distance required to write objectively about his past. For example, he is not afraid to show his younger self in a bad light:

This weird little creature had a voice and a precocious way of expressing himself which were marvellously irritating. [...] He was a tireless chatterer, a physical coward who lacked team spirit, a bright scholar who soon got bored and lazy, a terrible showoff [sic]. (*ibid.*: 286)

He also criticises his actions as a grown-up: "Christopher even stooped to the trick of cross-examining Richard one evening when he was drunk." (*ibid.*: 230) The narrator's objectivity adds to the text's authenticity, as does the fact that he sometimes quotes his brother to back up his statements (cf. *ibid.*: 198; 357), suggesting that he is not the only one holding certain views.

On the other hand, the narrator draws the reader's attention to the book's inauthenticity by freely admitting that he is only an interpreter of the material Kathleen and Frank have left him. In fact, he seems to regard his task as solving a "puzzle" (*ibid.*: 107) by examining each "clue" (*ibid.*: 79) closely. He concedes that some of the puzzle pieces are missing: "As Frank's letter of February 10th or 11th is lost, one doesn't know exactly what he wrote and can only guess at his motives for writing it." (*ibid.*: 172). As Isherwood never studied Kathleen's diary together with his mother (cf. *ibid.*: 2), he has to speculate rather a lot. Kathleen writes that "Mr Isherwood drove over and he and I drove to Chorley Hall. Had a great surprise. He asked me something so utterly unexpected." (*ibid.*: 44) She does not elaborate on this 'surprise' at all, but the narrator is of the opinion that Frank has just proposed to her (cf. *ibid.*: 45). This sort of self-censorship and regard for propriety even in her private journal makes it difficult to decode some of Kathleen's diary entries. She writes that she and Frank had a "sensible conversation" (*ibid.*: 47). According to the narrator, "[this] conversation and Kathleen's depression must have been about Frank's lack of money and the consequently dim prospects of their getting married soon." (*ibid.*) Later on, "Kathleen at length makes a direct though cryptic reference in her diary to her pregnancy: 'Told Mrs R. about 'August'.'" (*ibid.*: 191) Isherwood was born in August.

It is evident that the narrator holds a position of tremendous authority; for instance, he is capable of controlling the reader's attention: "Note how Frederick contradicts himself." (*ibid.*: 102) He has not only selected specific passages for the reader to see, but also dictates how they should be interpreted: "The first 'of course' seems to mean that Kathleen now regards The Child as a typical male hypocrite with a double standard." (*ibid.*: 35)

Furthermore, he reserves the right to judge his material: "Kathleen is seldom interesting when she writes about foreign travel: her diary keeps turning into a guidebook." (*ibid.*: 12) Isherwood's idea of 'interesting' seems to be the unique personal commentary one can make upon what one sees. Elsewhere, he remarks that "Kathleen seems to have behaved with great generosity throughout this humiliating affair." (*ibid.*: 37) By correcting her French (cf. *ibid.*: 250), he again situates himself above her diary.

The text's authenticity is undermined by this narrative construct, and Isherwood points out further deficiencies himself. When he says that "[t]his is the moment which Christopher's memory has chosen to retain" (*ibid.*: 289), he implies that the memory has a will of its own, that its subject cannot always control it. Another example is this next quote: "Christopher found himself taking part in (approximately) the following dialogue" (*ibid.*: 229). Isherwood admits he cannot fully remember everything that was said during this particular conversation – which is, of course, understandable. But why has he chosen to include this passage anyway?

. Isherwood remarks that "Kathleen kept rough drafts of the letters she wrote; the final versions, like nearly all the rest of her letters to Frank, have been lost or destroyed." (*ibid.*: 79) This not only proves that Isherwood has to speculate on what she might have written to Frank in order to elicit the replies he does have access to, but when the final letter has survived, he can compare it to the draft, and "her deletions are revealing" (*ibid.*). For example, she initially wrote and then struck through the sentence "Matrimony is such a frightful step for a woman." (*ibid.*: 80). This confirms that she regularly censored herself in her letters, and the final products, as well as Frank's letters, are therefore not an authentic picture of what their authors really thought at a given time.

Isherwood makes several references to Emily Brontë's *Wuthering Heights*. "When Christopher in his youth first read *Wuthering Heights* and Emily's poems, he at once superimposed their myth upon Wyberslegh" (*ibid.*: 179). Isherwood is placing his life into a literary context by suggesting that, not only are there geographical similarities between the two settings, but there are also parallels between his family and Brontë's characters. The families she portrays are trapped in a circle of tragedy from which none of the generations portrayed manages to break out of, with the exception, perhaps, of the last one. Interestingly, Kathleen regarded Frank's father as the squire of Marple (cf. *ibid.*: 183), just as Catherine Earnshaw is descended from a family of squires. There are numerous references to ancestral ghosts in Marple Hall (cf. *ibid.*: 221-230), another parallel to *Wuthering Heights*. Although he seems to consider Heathcliff a literary role model, Christopher claims he is "thankful that he isn't stuck, like Heathcliff, with Wuthering Heights and its tragedy. He is firmly resolved to die somewhere else" (*ibid.*: 180). However, he has only managed to free himself from his own family's influence by moving to another continent altogether (cf. *ibid.*: 362).

Isherwood places his life into the context of his own novels as well. He claims that the characters in *The Memorial* are based on his family, and he reveals which of his relatives appear in which disguises (cf. *ibid.*: 184-185). It seems as though Isherwood's novels were a mirror of reality, and *Kathleen and Frank* could well be equally as ambiguous in its juxtaposition of fact and fiction.

Furthermore, Isherwood draws the reader's attention to Kathleen's penchant for editing her own diary: "Against this entry – evidently many years later, for her handwriting has changed – Kathleen has written, 'Was introduced to Frank!'" (*ibid.*: 21) In "*The Baby's Progress*, a record of Christopher's growth and doings" (*ibid.*: 195), Kathleen reports that the young Christopher

> [w]*ill look at books for hours and likes being read to*... At two years old can string together quite long sentences, saying each word very carefully and distinctly. *His vocabulary very varied and large* [...] All through his childhood he never seemed at a loss for a word and was generally rather happy in his choice of words to best express his meaning. This last sentence can be seen, from the handwriting, to have been written in much later; so can the underlinings of the

sentences about looking at books and having a large vocabulary. They must be hindsighted references to Christopher's emergence as a writer. (*ibid.*: 201)

Although it is fascinating to analyse the significance of these modifications, the authenticity of Isherwood's sources is questionable.

Isherwood seems to have tried to give his family memoir a dramatic structure, especially towards the end of the book. He concludes a chapter with the following lines: "This is the moment which Christopher's memory has chosen to retain, not only as a picture but as a playback of Frank's voice. [...] He says, 'the order to mobilize has come'. His tone is quiet, gentle, almost reassuring. Then he is gone." (*ibid.*: 289) Isherwood clearly knows how to create suspense by foreshadowing future events (cf. *ibid.*: 156; 244; 275). The reader knows in advance that Frank will die in battle, and the chapters dealing with his involvement in the war as well as his subsequent death are structured in a very dramatic manner (cf. *ibid.*: 290-238). They are almost entirely without comment by the narrator, focusing instead on letters and, after Frank's disappearance, on Kathleen's diary, tracing the way she refers to her husband's death on its anniversary, even years later. This dramatic structure adds to the text's readability, but further limits its authenticity.

2.2.3. Promises Kept?

At this point, the idea that *Kathleen and Frank* focuses predominantly on Isherwood's parents seems unlikely. And indeed, it is contradicted explicitly in the afterword. Isherwood reveals that the reason why he decided to write this memoir was that when he was planning a series of lectures entitled "The Autobiography of My Books" in 1960, he realised that he did not know enough about his own past (cf. *ibid.*: 362). He decided to study his mother's diaries and his father's letters.

> While reading through these, Christopher saw how heredity and kinship create a woven fabric; its patterns vary, but its strands are the same throughout. Impossible to say exactly where Kathleen and Frank end and Richard and Christopher begin; they merge into each other. [...] Christopher has found that he is far more closely interwoven with Kathleen and Frank that he had supposed, or liked to believe. (*ibid.*: 362-363)

Now, Isherwood is fulfilling his parents' wish, in a way, and "their demand to be recorded is met by his eagerness to record" (*ibid.*). In an interview, he said that "[w]hen I started to write *Kathleen and Frank*, it was obvious to me that I couldn't tell their story without making my own gayness absolutely clear. So I kept stating this fact throughout the book." (Berg 2001: 108-109) The result is that

> *Kathleen and Frank* will seem at first to be their story rather than his. But the reader should remember *The Adventures of Mummy and Daddy*, that lost childhood work, and Kathleen's ironical comment on it [...]. Perhaps, on closer examination, this book too may prove to be chiefly about Christopher. (Isherwood 1971: 363)

Applying the concept of 'staged authenticity' to *Kathleen and Frank*, it can be said that although the excerpts from diaries and letters are quite authentic in their own right, they are relegated to the front region by the narrator's comments. The reader is like a tourist in someone else's life, and the narrator acts as a tour guide, steering the reader in the 'right' direction and revealing 'everything'. His comments could therefore be described as the back region.

From another perspective, the diaries and letters could be regarded as the back region, as they were originally not intended for publication, while the narrator's commentary was written with an audience in mind. But as the narrator also questions the reliability of his sources, the reader is unsure which material to trust in. This ambiguity reveals the staged nature of authenticity.

In fact, one can identify three layers of authenticity: first of all, the excerpts from diaries and letters, secondly, the narrator's commentary, and, finally, the meta-commentary, i.e. the narrator's remarks on the suitability and authenticity of his material. This layering is another indication that the book's authenticity is staged. The narrator is just as much of a tourist in his parents' lives, analysing their words and passing on his – obviously biased – interpretation to the reader.

2.3. Christopher and His Kind

Although, from a chronological viewpoint, this text could be regarded as a sequel of sorts to *Lions and Shadows*, the promise that Isherwood makes on the first page is radically different:

> There is a book called *Lions and Shadows*, published in 1938, which describes Christopher Isherwood's life between the ages of seventeen and twenty-four. It is not truly autobiographical, however. The author conceals important facts about himself. He overdramatizes many episodes and gives his characters fictitious names. In a foreword, he suggests that *Lions and Shadows* should be read as if it were a novel. The book I am now going to write will be as frank and factual as I can make it, especially as far as I myself am concerned. (Isherwood 2001: 1)

By contrasting this new text with *Lions and Shadows*, Isherwood affirms his sincerity, concrete proof of which is his ensuing admission: "To Christopher, Berlin meant boys." (*ibid.*: 2) This statement gives the reader the impression that Isherwood is going to reveal 'everything'. "At school, Christopher had fallen in love with many boys and been yearningly romantic about them. At college he had at last managed to get into bed with one." (*ibid.*: 3) David Garret Izzo has termed the book a "'now-the-truth-can-be-told' revisionist autobiography" (Izzo 2001: 252), and now that Isherwood is filling in the gaps within *Lions and Shadows*, the additional information he provides makes for a very different reading of this earlier work.

The subtitle of the original British edition, *1929-1939*, is comparable with a subtitle such as 'An Autobiography' or 'A Memoir'. It alone strongly suggests that the book in question is an autobiographical or even an historical account, and thus forms part of the autobiographical pact.

The narrator comments that "Christopher was quite willing to admit that his life in England was basically untruthful, since it conformed outwardly to standards of respectability which he inwardly rejected and despised." (Isherwood 2001: 7) This not only implies that there is an inner and an outer self – somewhat of a recurring theme in Isherwood's autobiographical works – but also that the reader is being permitted to see Christopher's inner self, which suggest authenticity.

2.3.1. Filling In the Gaps

As previously mentioned, *Mr Norris Changes Trains* and *Goodbye to Berlin* are based on Isherwood's experiences in Berlin. In *Christopher and His Kind*, he finally reveals "Christopher's real past" (*ibid.*: 41), and in order to convince the reader of the authenticity of this new account, Isherwood makes an effort to paint as complete a picture of the past as possible. He describes the Berlin of the 1930s (cf. *ibid.*: 29-30; 49) as well as the history of the Hirschfeld Institute at length (cf. *ibid.*: 17-19), even providing the reader with full addresses, such as "Nollendorfstraße 17[11]" (*ibid.*: 57; also cf. *ibid.*: 29; 49; 54). It is often Isherwood's exactness which lends credibility to the text. For example, he cites the brand names of the cigarettes and the beer he preferred (cf. *ibid.*: 22).

The text almost reads like a historical record, especially during the passages describing Hitler's rise to power and its effect on the atmosphere in the city (cf. *ibid.*: 113, 119-120, 122-125). These observations, though mostly unrelated to Isherwood himself, give credence to those which are. The reader is encouraged to think of the text as a 'history' of Isherwood's life, as though he were examining his own past through the same neutral historian's lens.

---

[11] In the Berlin of the present day, a plaque on the façade of Nollendorfstraße 17 still commemorates Isherwood's stay there from 1930-1933 – though it incorrectly states that he moved there in 1929.

While Isherwood's family is hardly mentioned at all in *Lions and Shadows*, there are numerous references to it in *Christopher and His Kind*, mostly regarding his difficult relationship with his mother: "Her will is the will of Nearly Everybody, and in their will is my death." (*ibid.*: 12) But with increasing maturity, he develops the ability to empathise with her, and his remarks become much more insightful. In 1936, he records the following in his diary:

> It is amazing—the barrier, even now, between us. Mostly of shyness. [...] She is infinitely more broadminded, more reasonable, than she was in the old days—I like talking to her, in fact I talk to her better and more amusingly than to anyone else; but the ice is never really broken. (*ibid.*: 247-248)

This 'barrier' between them is evidenced by the fact that Kathleen is always referred to by her name; she is never 'Christopher's mother'.

A great deal of the book incorporates elements of confessional literature. While *Lions and Shadows* focuses on Isherwood's emergence as a writer, *Christopher and His Kind* tells the story of his coming-of-age as a homosexual. After his "first—and last—complete sex experience with a woman" (*ibid.*: 10),

> [h]e asked himself: Do I now want to go to bed with more women and girls? Of course not, as long as I can have boys. Why do I prefer boys? Because of their shape and their voices and their smell and the way they move. And boys can be romantic. I can put them into my myth and fall in love with them. Girls can be absolutely beautiful but never romantic. [...] Couldn't you get yourself excited by the shape of girls, too—if you worked hard at it? Perhaps. And couldn't you invent another myth—to put girls into? Why the hell should I? Well, it would be a lot more convenient for you, if you did. Then you wouldn't have all these problems. Society would accept you. You wouldn't be out of step with nearly everybody else. It was at this point in his self-examination that Christopher would become suddenly, blindly furious. Damn Nearly Everybody. (*ibid.*: 11-12)

This passage appears like a dialogue between two conflicting selves within Isherwood, in which one is the more pragmatic and sensible, and the other is the more passionate and rebellious self. This 'inner voice' lends authenticity to the text, just as it does in *Lions and Shadows* (cf. Isherwood 1996: 187-188).

While Isherwood never wavered in his decision, there are also several references to the sort of prejudices other people had against homosexuals, even people he worked with (cf. Isherwood 2001: 157-158; 160-162; 163). That is why Christopher's "tribe" (*ibid.*: 126) is all the more important to him. "Up to now, he had behaved as though the tribe didn't exist and homosexuality were a private way of life discovered by himself and a few friends." (*ibid.*: 16) In *Lions and Shadows*, the narrator talks of his alienation from the "Other Side" (Isherwood 1996: 70), i.e. the 'Poshocracy'. In *Christopher and His Kind*, the term 'The Others' seems to stand for the "dictatorship" (Isherwood 2001: 207) of the heterosexual majority.

It is the feeling of belonging to a group of people that gives Isherwood strength, and he feels a strong loyalty to his tribe: "It was like a lack of oxygen; his nature gasped for the atmosphere of his fellow tribesmen. As never before, he realized that they were all his brothers—yes, even those who denied their brotherhood and betrayed it" (*ibid.*: 163). "He must never again give way to embarrassment, never deny the rights of his tribe, never apologize for its existence" (*ibid.*: 334-335). Their shared sexual tastes was also one of the strengths of Isherwood's friendship with W.H. Auden; in 1936 he wrote in his diary that

> although I was often very much annoyed by his fussing and by the mess he made—still I never for one moment was more than annoyed. I never felt opposed to him in my deepest being—as I sometimes feel opposed to almost everyone I know. We are, after all, of the same sort. (*ibid.*: 240)

In the course of the book, there is a development from Christopher's sexual promiscuity to his first serious relationship with a young boy named Heinz:

> Christopher had no hesitation in falling in love with Heinz. It seemed most natural to him that they two should be drawn together. [...] He wasn't yet aware that he was letting himself in for a relationship which would be far more serious than any he had had in his life. (*ibid.*: 91)

Their relationship ended with Heinz's arrest by Nazi authorities, after which

> Christopher's widowerhood lent glamour to his image. If Christopher had been parted from a wife, a few sympathetic girls would have been touched by his plight and asked themselves, 'Couldn't I make him happy again?' In Christopher's case, the sympathizers were young men who asked the same question. He encouraged them all to try. (*ibid.*: 290-291)

It is this unapologetic attitude that is characteristic of the text. There are several passages which were probably rather shocking to the original audience, such as offhand comments like: "[o]r he is suffering from diarrhea or worried by rectal bleeding." (*ibid.*: 139) Most of these revelations refer to Isherwood's sexuality: "What excited Christopher most, a struggle which turned gradually into a sex act, seemed perfectly natural to these German boys; indeed, it excited them too." (*ibid.*: 31) In an attempt to discern the reason for his infatuation with blond boys, he writes that

> Christopher chose to identify himself with a black-haired British ancestor and to see the Blond as the invader who comes from another land to conquer and rape him. Thus the Blond becomes the masculine foreign *yang* mating with Christopher's feminine native *yin*... (*ibid.*: 4)

Later on in the text, Isherwood elaborates on his theory of the *yin* versus the *yang*, while simultaneously revealing more about his sexual tastes:

> When I say that Viertel needed a victim, I mean a willing victim and a victim who could thrive on victimization. My theory is that Viertel's ideal victim could only have been a male

homosexual—and not just any male homosexual but one who, like Christopher, was able to enjoy both the *yang* and the *yin* role in sex. (*ibid.*: 153)

It is clear that Isherwood *wants* to shock his audience; after all, as the author, he has the power to decide what the reader sees. Isherwood himself admits that Christopher was quite "aggressive" (*ibid.*: 335) in his homosexuality. In his work *October*, published in collaboration with Don Bachardy, he says "whether we like it or not, our unique act of self-expression is a sexual act" (Isherwood 1981: 81), which means that, for him, recounting memories of a sexual nature is akin to establishing his identity as a homosexual.

Isherwood not only reveals (potentially) embarrassing facts about himself, such as that he once caught Gonorrhoea (cf. Isherwood 2001: 329), but also a few anecdotes referring to his friends: "Wystan had to undergo an operation for a rectal fissure. [He] suffered from the aftereffects [sic] of this operation for several years. They inspired him to write his 'Letter to a Wound,' which forms part of *The Orators*." (*ibid.*: 39-40) He remembers that his friend

> Francis seldom actually needed waking. Usually, Christopher would find him reading and smoking, propped on pillows, on the outer side of his bed. On the inner side, snuggled against the wall, the back of the head of a boy would be visible. And sometimes another boy would be asleep on the couch, under a pile of coats and rugs. (*ibid.*: 23)

Isherwood heightens the text's authenticity by breaking taboos. He reveals some very private details about his life, suggesting to the reader that he is permitting them to see his true self.

2.3.2. The Narrator's Critical Attitude

In *Christopher and His Kind*, the narrator is characterised by a pronounced critical attitude, both towards his past self and towards his sources and life-writing in general.

As a first-person narrator, he looks back on a former self that he calls 'Christopher'. This dichotomy is established on the first page of the narrative, on which the 'I' narrator contrasts himself with the "twenty-four-year-old Christopher" (*ibid.*: 1).

According to Philippe Lejeune's study "Autobiography in the Third Person", this type of life-writing is fairly rare (cf. Lejeune 1977: 46). Isherwood "speaks about himself *as if* another were speaking about him, or as if he himself were speaking of another" (*ibid.*: 29), while the reader "continues to read [the book] as first-person discourse" (*ibid.*). According to Lejeune, although the text is still subject to the rules of the autobiographical pact (cf. *ibid.*), the fact that the protagonist is referred to as 'Christopher' carries autobiography into the sphere of "fictive fiction" (*ibid.*: 34).

The narrator emphasises the distance between himself and his past self by analysing Christopher's behaviour in an almost scientific manner:

> What did Christopher think Wilfrid condemned him for? I believe Christopher suspected that Wilfrid was a severely repressed homosexual and that, as such, he condemned Christopher for his aggressive frankness about his own sex life. If Christopher did indeed suspect this, it would have been characteristic of him to be extra frank with Wilfrid, in order to jolt him into frankness about himself. (Isherwood 2001: 71)

It appears as though he regarded his immature younger self as a different person altogether: "It seems extraordinary to me, now, that Christopher would have so far exposed himself as to let her see that Otto was 'a cause of misery' to him" (*ibid*.: 80). "I don't agree with the majority of Christopher's choices, now." (*ibid*.: 118) His detached attitude suggests that he can write about his past life with sufficient objectivity as to be entirely truthful, affirming both his sincerity and the authenticity of his account. He thus holds a position of considerable authority.

In fact, Isherwood suggests that there were several personas within Christopher: "I don't blame Christopher the amateur observer for his lack of foresight. I do condemn Christopher the novelist for not having taken a psychological interest, long before this, in the members of the Nazi high command." (*ibid*: 120) This dissociation of the self can be compared to the struggle between the protagonist and 'Isherwood the Artist' in *Lions and Shadows*.

Further proof of Isherwood's sincerity is the fact that he does not hesitate to show himself in a bad light. He admits that "Stephen [Spender] had to endure Christopher's moods, his hypochondria, his sulks, and his domestic crises" (*ibid*.: 55). Isherwood often mentions Christopher's arrogance (cf. *ibid*.: 69; 105; 152) and criticises the fact that he "was utterly unable to believe in moral attitudes other than his own" (*ibid*.: 261). He communicates his maturity by looking back on his past actions and interpreting them in a new light:

> That evening, a party of silly Brazilian girls declared brightly, in Heinz's presence, that they hated all Germans. Christopher got up and walked out of the lounge. He enjoyed making such gestures of righteous indignation but didn't pause to consider how much Heinz must be embarrassed by them. (*ibid*.: 226)

In his diary he records his sometimes conflicting feelings for Auden: "In China I sometimes found myself really hating him [...]. I was meanly jealous of him, too. Jealous of his share of the limelight; jealous because he'll no longer play the role of dependent, admiring younger brother." (*ibid*.: 304) This self-critical stance ingratiates him with the reader; the fact that he is aware of his faults and not afraid to talk about them is an indication of his sincerity. He presents a complete and thus authentic picture of his personality.

The benefits of the third-person perspective also include the freedom for Isherwood to cite other people's praise without seeming immodest. For example, he quotes Cyril Connolly, who referred to Christopher "in print as 'a hope of English fiction'" (*ibid.*: 271), as well as flattering comments from E.M. Forster (cf. *ibid.*: 105) and W. Somerset Maugham (cf. *ibid.*: 326-327). In her essay on Gertrude Stein's *The Autobiography of Alice B. Toklas*, Lynn Z. Bloom identifies the lack of need for false modesty as one of the advantages of writing about oneself in the third person (cf. Bloom 1978: 88) – although Stein did this in a different way. According to Bloom, the third-person construct distracts the reader from the "egotism inherent in conventional autobiography" (*ibid.*: 83), and the control this affords the writer over their material extends to the self-image they want to present.

However, the fact that the narrator and the protagonist almost seem like different beings creates some problems as well. While it permits Isherwood a certain objectivity and freedom of expression, it could also be interpreted as an indication that he is uncomfortable with telling the truth about himself, and that he does not dare do so as a first-person narrator. There is no unity of self in this construct, which diminishes the text's authenticity, as Isherwood is not being entirely true to himself. According to Hart, "only a continuity of identity of being makes the autobiographical act or purpose meaningful" (Hart 1970: 500).

The division of narrator and protagonist is broken, however, when both appear in one sentence: "[H]ere I am confronted by the reality of Christopher's monster behavior—his tears followed by cold calculation—and it shocks me, it hurts my self-esteem, even after all these years!" (Isherwood 2001: 145) "Christopher's first visit to Berlin was short—a week or ten days—but that was sufficient; I now recognize it as one of the decisive events of my life." (*ibid.*: 3) In these passages, Isherwood reverts to a continuous model of selfhood.

As before, Isherwood deconstructs authenticity even while he creates it. After all, he merely promises that the book will be "as frank and factual as I can make it, especially as far as I myself am concerned" (*ibid*: 1), which proves that he is still conscious of the limitations of the autobiographical genre.

Throughout the text, the reader is reminded of the memory's fallibility: "After this, there is a gap in Christopher's diary and a blank in my mind." (*ibid.*: 190) "My own memory records nothing. Christopher must have found this gradual parting painful and therefore chosen to forget it." (*ibid.*: 330) The fact that a lot of time has passed since the events described took place is also emphasised:

> I wish I could remember what impression Jean Ross—the real-life original of Sally Bowles in
> *Goodbye to Berlin*—made on Christopher when they first met. But I can't. Art has transfigured

life and other people's art has transfigured Christopher's art. What remains with me from those early years is almost entirely Sally [...] And both Sally and Jean keep being jostled to one side of my memory to make way for the actresses who have played the part of Sally on the stage and on the screen. (*ibid.*: 60)

This suggests once more that, even in Isherwood's memory, the line between fact and fiction is blurred. Elsewhere, Isherwood implies that some of his memories could potentially be false: "I have a memory connected with this which I suspect. It isn't recorded in Christopher's diary and it is rather too symbolic to be strictly true" (*ibid.*: 311). Some sensory memories are presented as all the more durable: "I can still make myself faintly feel the delicious nausea of initiation terror which Christopher felt as Wystan pushed back the heavy leather door curtain of a boy bar called the Cosy Corner." (*ibid.*: 3)

Isherwood admits that he burned the diary he kept during his time in Berlin, as "it was full of details about his sex life" (*ibid.*: 41). Covering the missing years, Isherwood has to rely on the letters of others, even though they are largely undated (cf. *ibid.*). Some important letters are lost (cf. *ibid.*: 113), others "ring shockingly false" (*ibid.*: 94). By acknowledging these limiting factors, Isherwood confirms his sincerity, but who is to say that any other sources he is basing his accounts on are not flawed as well?

He also quotes from his mother's diary (cf. *ibid.*: 40; 80; 247-248), his "most reliable source of information" (*ibid.*: 41) on this period. Furthermore, there are excerpts from some of his friends' autobiographies, such as Stephen Spender's *World within World* (cf. *ibid.*: 54-55; 56; 67; 106-107), John Lehmann's *The Whispering Gallery* (cf. *ibid.*: 96-97) and Gerald Hamilton's *Mr. Norris and I* (cf. *ibid.*: 73). Although their versions of events award the reader with a fresh perspective on Isherwood, he has obviously chosen those passages he wants the reader to see. More importantly, the memories he has selected have already been transformed into narrative by his friends, which proves how unreliable they are.

Isherwood held on to the diary he kept from 1933 onwards, but the authenticity of this document is questionable as well: "I've had enough of this. I'm tired of writing this discreet literary little journal, with one eye on the landscape and the other on the Hogarth Press." (*ibid.*: 141) Isherwood exposes his tendency to censor himself and to falsify diary entries: "That last long pompously false sentence is produced by Christopher's feeling that he ought to make some statement befitting the importance of the situation." (*ibid.*: 134) "In this mirror of a diary, Christopher reveals a few frank glimpses of himself. The rest is posing." (*ibid.*: 290)

It is remarkable how many parallels Isherwood draws to his novels. This is especially the case with *Goodbye to Berlin*; he reveals which acquaintance each of the characters was inspired by and how the fictional character differs from the original (cf. *ibid.*: 41-46; 50-53; 64-65; 66-

72). He uncovers how they were "[i]n real life" (*ibid.*: 63; 64; 67), which suggests authenticity. On the other hand, there is a passage in which he says that he has "no verbatim record of what [Jean Ross] said. The best I can do is to report it in the style of Sally Bowles" (*ibid.*: 149). This means that, after disclosing what happened 'in real life', he is now reverting to his usage of fictionalised characters to describe 'reality' – another indicator of how blurred the line between fact and fiction is for the narrator.

Isherwood also includes several extended passages on novels he planned or partly wrote but never published, such as 'The Lost' (cf. *ibid.*: 175-178) and 'Paul Is Alone' (cf. *ibid.*: 208-212). It is remarkable to see how much these works resemble his own life, either in terms of plot or in terms of the themes which are addressed. In fact, Isherwood admits that "Like *The Lost*, *Paul Is Alone* was an attempt by Christopher to pack a section of his past life into a plot structure" (*ibid.*: 212). It is clear by now that these were not the only times he did this.

As before, Isherwood's foreshadowing adds a dramatic quality to the text: "[T]his proved to have been a fatally silly piece of advice" (*ibid.*: 136). He has the ability to look back on his life and to point out which encounters proved especially meaningful in hindsight:

> If Christopher and Heinz didn't say goodbye to Erwin on this occasion, they were fated never to do so. [...] Someone told me that he was arrested by the Nazis and died in a concentration camp, but I haven't been able to confirm this. I only know that he is dead now. (*ibid.*: 145-146)

The book ends with a glimpse of the future as well:

> This is where I leave Christopher, at the rail, looking eagerly, nervously, hopefully toward the land where he will spend more than half of his life. [...] I will allow him and Wystan to ask one question—I can already guess what it is—and I will answer it: Yes, my dears, each of you will find the person you came here to look for [...]. You, Wystan, will find him very soon, within three months. You, Christopher, will have to wait much longer for yours. [...] At present, he is only four years old. (*ibid.*: 339)

Isherwood clearly knows how to stage a dramatic ending. The text's authenticity is deconstructed by his usage of devices usually employed in fiction.

2.3.3. Promises Kept?

The way in which Isherwood directly contrasts the story of his life as laid out in *Lions and Shadows* with 'what really happened' suggests that the former work is really the front region, while *Christopher and His Kind* is now permitting the reader a look behind the scenes, revealing the private rather than the social. Within the text, the comments from the more mature, present-day first-person narrator could be described as still more authentic, a sort of 'back-of-the-backstage' view. These comments are even more honest, uncovering the real motives behind Christopher's diary entries and letters. However, the very fact that Isherwood goes beyond this earlier work stages authenticity. The reader is left with a sneaking suspicion: if Isherwood completely revised one autobiographical account and replaced it with another, who is to say that he will not be doing the same with *Christopher and His Kind* in a few years?

Furthermore, there are also a few remaining gaps in the narrative, mostly due to Isherwood's continued use of fictitious names (cf. *ibid.*: 32; 42; 220; 314). He always informs the reader of this beforehand, by saying, for example, "Christopher met a youth whom I shall call Bubi (Baby)[12]" (*ibid.*: 4). This strengthens his claim for sincerity, but the fact remains that the reader is aware there exists a back region which they are not permitted to enter. Interestingly, Isherwood refers to Stephen Spender's partner as "Jimmy Younger" (*ibid.*: 220), which is the same name that Spender uses in his autobiography *World within World* (1951). Spender speaks of Edward Upward as 'Allen Chalmers', the fictitious name Isherwood invented for him in *Lions and Shadows*. Considering that Upward himself used this name as a pseudonym when he published a short story set in Mortmere entitled "The Railway Accident" (1949), this sheds some light on the power of writing.

Isherwood also confesses to the existence of a public 'Isherwood persona':

> Wystan was embarrassed by Christopher's public self—the Isherwood who would put an arm around his shoulder when cameras or other eyes were watching. Isherwood was good at self-exposure; he knew all the tricks of modesty and never boasted except in private. (*ibid.*: 332)

The narrator evidently regards 'Christopher' and 'Isherwood' as different beings, and it is the latter who enjoys the attention of a camera (cf. *ibid.*: 294) and who loves "playing to the gallery" (*ibid.*: 53; 58). Admitting that he is longing for a partner to whom he can reveal himself fully and with whom he does not have to pretend (cf. *ibid.*: 339), he hints at the fact that, just as touristic experiences can be staged, *Christopher and His Kind* is really nothing more than an artistic work specifically designed to show the reader the person, or *a* person, behind "Christopher's public self" (*ibid.*: 332).

Michael Ratcliffe summarised the book eloquently in *The Times*, describing it as "a striptease on chosen ground. Strip [Isherwood] does—with energy, elegance and wit—but he teases, too." (Ratcliffe 1977: 17)

---

[12] Incidentally, this translation is incorrect. It is unclear whether Isherwood was aware of this or not.

3. The Serpentine Quality of Fiction

To what extent is it possible at all to produce a fully authentic text? As mentioned above, in autobiography, memories are filtered twice, first through the author's subjectivity, and then by the process of writing them down. That is why, according to Trilling, narrative can never be authentic. It is an attempt to forge causalities and to assign a beginning and an end to a series of events which did not exist in real life (cf. Trilling 1974: 135). Trilling describes the "narrative past [as] the very type of inauthenticity" (*ibid.*: 139). However, for an autobiography to be appealing to the reader, he or she has to feel that it portrays some sort of 'truth'. Consequently, the author has to stage authenticity.

Isherwood does this by providing documentary evidence, by being very exact, and by adding points of view different to his own. Whenever he addresses private matters and breaks taboos, which is mostly the case in *Kathleen and Frank* and *Christopher and His Kind*, the reader is led to believe that he is not holding back any information about himself. There is also a marked difference between the narrator and the protagonist, especially in the case of *Christopher and His Kind*, in which a first-person narrator looks back on a third-person past self. The narrator's maturity signals that he can talk about his life in an objective manner. Adopting a critical stance towards his past self indicates that he is truly sincere; he does not only present positive aspects of his personality, but seems true to his real self – the very definition of authenticity.

However, the construction of authenticity is accompanied by a simultaneous deconstruction. Isherwood admits that there are limitations to the autobiographical genre, highlighting gaps in his memory and conceding that essential sources are missing. All three works also share a high degree of intertextuality; by including details from his novels and contrasting them with what happened "in real life" (Isherwood 2001: 67), Isherwood confronts the reader with the similarities between 'fact' and 'fiction'. He also draws the reader's attention to falsified or self-censored diary entries. Although this speaks for the narrator's sincerity, the reader now has reason to question the texts' authenticity. By shaping his accounts in a dramatic way, for example by foreshadowing certain important events, Isherwood further diminishes their verisimilitude. Interestingly, although these books are very different from each other with regard to their contents and to their purposes as expressed in the author's promises, this construction and deconstruction of authenticity is present in each of them.

As these autobiographical works essentially form a series, the reader assumes that they gradually reveal more, that the latest shows the most authentic picture of the author's life. This is true to some extent; for example, the comments in *Lions and Shadows* concerning the protagonist's feelings about war and about the 'Truly Strong Man' will remain rather obscure to the reader until they read the additional information provided by *Kathleen and Frank* about Isherwood's parental heritage. While these gaps hint at the existence of a back region in *Lions and Shadows*, it is not shown to the reader, who, while reading the book, feels that something is missing. This is why *Lions and Shadows* seems to be purely front region, concentrating on Isherwood's public role as a writer and revealing hardly anything of a private nature.

In *Kathleen and Frank*, on the other hand, the reader is led to believe that he or she is now being led backstage. Within the book, the documentary material, i.e. the letters and diary excerpts, form the front region, while the narrator's commentary presents the reader with a view beyond these documents. He analyses dishonest behaviour and uncovers Kathleen's tendency to censor herself in both her diary and her letters. However, as an interpreter of their actions and words, the narrator is just as much of a tourist in Kathleen's and Frank's lives as the reader, which is why the authenticity of his remarks is staged. Alternatively, the diaries and letters could also be regarded as the back region, as, unlike the commentary, they were never composed for publication. This ambiguity is confusing to the reader and draws attention once more to the staged nature of authenticity.

Isherwood explicitly contrasts *Christopher and His Kind* with *Lions and Shadows*, which he considers to be an incomplete account of the years leading up to his move to Berlin. *Lions and Shadows* is thus relegated to the front region, while in *Christopher and His Kind*, the back region, the author appears to reveal everything. Within the latter text, the first-person narrator exposes his former self's mistakes and vanities, presenting a 'back-of-the-backstage' view, as it were. The fact that *Christopher and His Kind* goes beyond *Lions and Shadows* in itself stages authenticity.

Considering the inherent inauthenticity of narrative, it is impossible to fulfil the promise of the autobiographical pact. This is evidenced by Isherwood's works. Of the three books, *Lions and Shadows* is the one which imitates the generic markers of autobiography most closely; for example, it is the only one which is narrated in the first person throughout. That is why there is less need for it to construct authenticity. Neither a traditional *künstlerroman* nor a true autobiography, it is between genres. This is confirmed by the various ways it has been referred to by others: a "fictionalized memoir" (Berg 2007: 3), an "autobiographical sketch" (Spender 1977: 132), or even an "autobiographical-historical parable[…]" (Hynes 1976: 322). Most reviewers at the time of publication commented on Isherwood's confusion of purpose (cf. Finney 1976: 130); for example, the *Times Literary Supplement* reviewer wrote:

> What it is not is what is was intended to be—an objective account of "an Education in the Twenties" of a young English novelist. What it is, more than anything, is an intensely personal, subjective account of Mr. Isherwood's own adolescent trials and tribulations. (Hayward 1938: 185)

Isherwood himself urges the reader to regard the book as fiction, and he even provides them with a definition of what a novel should be: "a contraption—like a motor bicycle, whose action depends upon the exactly co-ordinated working of all its inter-related parts" (Isherwood 1996: 159). Using this metaphor, one could say that *Lions and Shadows* is not entirely convincing as a novel. The 'parts' do not fit, and several pieces are missing altogether.

To a certain extent, in *Kathleen and Frank*, the autobiographical pact is established via the title – the book supposedly tells the story of these two late-Victorian people. Isherwood promises that the text he is presenting is both authentic and relevant. At first, it seems as though he were fulfilling his promise; he includes a wealth of documentary material and even lets the protagonists speak for themselves. The third-person perspective appears to award the narrator the objectivity required to portray Kathleen's and Frank's lives in an authentic manner. But more and more, it becomes evident that the real protagonist, and the true subject of the book, is Isherwood himself. Revealing his homosexuality, the narrator steps into the foreground, and the promise made at the beginning of the text is not kept, as Isherwood himself admits in the afterword.

In *Christopher and His Kind*, the autobiographical pact is very simple: the account will be "as frank and factual as [Isherwood] can make it" (Isherwood 2001: 1), at least as far as he himself is concerned. He purports to uncover everything which was unclear before: his family, his sexuality, and the particulars of his 'real' life in Berlin. The text reads like a confession, with Isherwood criticising his younger self, 'Christopher', quite harshly. At the same time, however, he admits to gaps in his memory, to missing documents as well as to falsified letters and diary entries. His material is not as authentic as the reader would prefer it to be. Furthermore, recounting the plots and themes of his novels, Isherwood blurs the line between fact and fiction to such an extent that it is unclear what really happened and what did not.

Each of the books also appears to be an attempt at self-reinvention or self-fashioning, at Isherwood giving his life a plot. While in *Lions and Shadows*, he explores his self as an artist, in *Kathleen and Frank*, he examines the role of family in constructing the self. In *Christopher and His Kind*, he establishes himself as a homosexual and as a member of his 'tribe'.

Isherwood seems to transgress against the conventions of autobiography in order to show that the genre's apparent authenticity is staged. Eakin confirms that "the self that is the center of all autobiographical narrative is necessarily a fictive structure" (Eakin 1985: 3). In Isherwood's works, this is indicated by the struggle between different selves, for example between "Isherwood the Artist" (Isherwood 1996: 187) and his "familiar everyday self" (*ibid.*: 165), or between his inner and outer self (cf. Isherwood 2001: 7). In both *Kathleen and Frank* and *Christopher and His Kind*, the narrator speaks of his past identity in such a way as to suggest a certain dissociation of the self.

According to Eakin, "the materials of the past are shaped by memory and imagination to serve the needs of the present consciousness" (Eakin 1985: 5). In Isherwood's case, these needs include the desire to break out of something. In *Lions and Shadows*, for example, by simply not mentioning his family at all, Isherwood appears to be trying to break loose from his parents' influence. The same is attempted in *Kathleen and Frank*, but after having written the book, he has come to the conclusion that this is simply not possible. Instead, Isherwood now has the ability to forgive himself for the way he behaved towards his mother, and ultimately, the text could be regarded as an act of redemption.

In her review of *Christopher and His Kind*, Gabriele Annan claims that looking at Isherwood's oeuvre in its entirety one can see that, "one way or another, first as an act of defiance and then as a fight for equal rights, it has always been a homosexual campaign" (Annan 1977: 401). Prior to the Sexual Offences Act 1967, Isherwood was forced to carry out this campaign in a covert manner, lest he should implicate himself in then illegal acts. However, looking closely at the text, it is evident that he went as far as possible without getting into legal trouble. The reason why he did not reveal the narrators of *Mr Norris Changes Trains* and *Goodbye to Berlin* as homosexual was because he thought it would defeat their purpose as inconspicuous observers and as foils for the other characters (cf. Berg 2001: 76). In *Kathleen and Frank*, Isherwood finally came out in print, and it is his unapologetic frankness that made him a symbol for the Californian gay-rights movement. In *Christopher and His Kind*, there are several passages which, unusually for the time, convey the message that homosexual relationships are no different from heterosexual ones. Asked by Cyril Connolly, how he felt about Heinz, "Christopher replied casually but nastily: 'Oh, very much as you feel about [your wife], I suppose.'" (Isherwood 2001: 272) He remarks that, at times, he and Heinz "were absurdly like the most ordinary happily married heterosexual couple" (*ibid.*: 92).

Isherwood is not the only novelist who used his works to express scepticism towards the autobiographical genre. Stephen Spender claims that we "colour our past experiences with those present ones which give them significance, illustrating what we are and not what they were" (Spender 1977: 322). Hemingway invites the reader to regard *A Moveable Feast* as fiction, should he or she so wish (cf. Hemingway 1964: n.p.), and Yeats admits that although he has changed nothing to his knowledge in his autobiographies, he has potentially changed a lot of things without being aware of it (cf. Yeats 1999: 39). According to Cecil Day Lewis,

> everyone, through the inner monologue that is his reflective commentary on experience, selects and subtly distorts the facts so as to make him more interesting or more tolerable to himself, in doing so he creates a personal mythology which, because it modifies him, does become representative truth. (Day Lewis 1960: 243)

However, while most writers have disregarded their doubts and published more or less straight autobiography anyway, Isherwood has used his artistic licence to play with the conventions of life-writing, showing the reader that it can never be authentic.

But if the value of authenticity is deconstructed, what has taken its place instead? Isherwood once said:

> I've always felt very little difference between fiction and non-fiction. What matters is what you say about a given situation. Maybe you can explain its reality better by heightening its drama, by way of a comment on it. Fiction enters the garden in a serpentine way. (Berg 2001: 182)

It seems that, according to Isherwood, it is art which has replaced authenticity.

Bibliography

Abbott, Porter H. "Autobiography, Autography, Fiction: Groundwork for a Taxonomy of Textual Categories." *New Literary History* 19.3 (1988): 597-615.

Annan, Gabriele. "The Issyvoo Years." *Times Literary Supplement* 1 April 1977: 401.

Berg, James J. Introduction. *Isherwood on Writing*. By Christopher Isherwood. Ed. James J. Berg. Minneapolis: U of Minnesota P, 2007. 1-33.

Berg, James J., and Chris Freeman, eds. *Conversations with Christopher Isherwood*. Jackson, WI: UP of Mississippi, 2001.

---, eds. *The Isherwood Century. Essays on the Life and Work of Christopher Isherwood*. Madison: U of Wisconsin P, 2001.

Bloom, Lynn. "Gertrude Is Alice Is Everybody: Innovation and Point of View in Gertrude Stein's Autobiographies." *Twentieth Century Literature* 24.1 (1978): 81-93.

Bolton, Jonathan. "Mid-Term Autobiography and the Second World War." *Journal of Modern Literature* 30.1 (2006): 155-172.

Brontë, Emily. *Wuthering Heights*. 1847. Ed. Ian Jack. Oxford: Oxford UP, 1985.

Bruner, Jerome. "The Narrative Construction of Reality." *Critical Inquiry* 18.1 (1991): 1-21.

Bruss, Elizabeth. *Autobiographical Acts. The Changing Situation of a Literary Genre*. Baltimore: John Hopkins UP, 1976.

Connolly, Cyril. *Enemies of Promise*. 1938. London: André Deutsch, 1988.

Cuddon, J.A. *A Dictionary of Literary Terms and Literary Theory*. 4th ed. Rev. by C.E. Preston. Oxford: Blackwell Publishers, 1998.

Cunningham, Valentine. *British Writers of the Thirties*. Oxford: Oxford UP, 1988.

Day Lewis, C. *The Buried Day*. 1960. London: Chatto & Windus, 1969.

De Man, Paul. "Autobiography as De-Facement." *MLN* 94.5 (1979): 919-930.

Eakin, Paul John. *Fictions in Autobiography. Studies in the Art of Self-Invention*. Princeton: Princeton UP, 1985.

---. Foreword. *On Autobiography*. By Philippe Lejeune. Minneapolis: U of Minnesota P, 1989.

---. *Touching the World. Reference in Autobiography*. Princeton: Princeton UP, 1992.

Finney, Brian. *Christopher Isherwood. A Critical Biography*. London: Faber and Faber, 1979.

---. "Laily, Mortmere and All That." *Twentieth Century Literature* 22.3 (1976): 286-302.

Grigson, Geoffrey. "Education in the Twenties." *New Verse* 29 (1938): 18-19.

Hamilton, Gerald. *Mr. Norris and I. An Autobiographical Sketch*. London: Allan Wingate, 1956.

Hart, Francis H. "Notes for an Anatomy of Modern Autobiography." *New Literary History* 1.3 (1970): 485-511.

Hayward, John Davy. "Novelist's Youth." *Times Literary Supplement* 19 March 1938: 185.

Hemingway, Ernest. Preface. *A Moveable Feast*. By Hemingway. New York: Charles Scribner's Sons, 1964. n.p.

Hynes, Samuel. *The Auden Generation. Literature and Politics in England in the 1930s*. London: The Bodley Head, 1976.

Isherwood, Christopher. *The Berlin Novels*. 1971. London: Minerva, 1992.

---. *Christopher and His Kind*. 1976. Minneapolis: U of Minnesota P, 2001.

---. *Kathleen and Frank*. London: Methuen, 1971.

---. *Lions and Shadows. An Education in the Twenties*. 1938. London: Minerva, 1996.

Isherwood, Christopher, and Don Bachardy. *October*. 1980. Los Angeles: Twelvetrees Press, 1981.

Izzo, David Garrett. *Christopher Isherwood. His Era, His Gang, and the Legacy of the Truly Strong Man*. Columbia: U of South Carolina P, 2001.

Joyce, James. *A Portrait of the Artist as a Young Man*. 1916. London: Penguin, 1996.

Lehmann, John. *The Whispering Gallery. Autobiography I*. London: Longmans, Green & Co., 1955.

Lejeune, Philippe. "Autobiography in the Third Person." Trans. Annette and Edward Tomarken. *New Literary History* 9.1 (1977): 27-50.

---. *On Autobiography*. Trans. Katherine Leary. Minneapolis: U of Minnesota P, 1989.

MacCannell, Dean. "Staged Authenticity: Arrangements of Social Space in Tourist Settings." *The American Journal of Sociology* 79.3 (1973): 589-603.

Milnes, Tim, and Kerry Sinanan, eds. *Romanticism, Sincerity and Authenticity*. Basingstoke: Palgrave Macmillan, 2010.

Mullan, John. "True Stories." *The Guardian*. 27 October 2007. http://www.guardian.co.uk/books/2007/oct/27/jeanettewinterson (last accessed 27 February 2011).

Neisser, Ulric, and Robyn Fivush, eds. *The Remembering Self. Construction and Accuracy in the Self-Narrative*. Cambridge: Cambridge UP, 1994.

Olney, James, ed. *Autobiography: Essays Theoretical and Critical*. Princeton: Princeton UP, 1980.

Parker, Peter. *Isherwood: A Life*. London: Picador, 2004.

---. "Isherwood, Christopher William Bradshaw (1904–1986)." *Oxford Dictionary of National Biography*. 2004. http://www.oxforddnb.com/view/article/39833 (last accessed 27 Feb 2011).

Piazza, Paul. *Christopher Isherwood. Myth and Anti-Myth*. New York: Columbia UP, 1978.

Pike, Burton. "Time in Autobiography." *Comparative Literature* 28.4 (1976): 326-342.

Ratcliffe, Michael. "Herr Issyvoo in His Element." *The Times* 31 March 1977: 17.

Rose, Jean. "RE: question about Kathleen and Frank by Christopher Isherwood." E-mail to the author. 18 February 2011.

Spender, Stephen. *World within World*. 1951. London: Faber and Faber, 1977.

Trilling, Lionel. *Sincerity and Authenticity*. 1972. Oxford: Oxford UP, 1974.

Weintraub, Karl J. "Autobiography and Historical Consciousness." *Critical Inquiry* 1.4 (1975): 821-848.

Yeats, W.B. *Autobiographies*. The Collected Works of W.B. Yeats, Volume III. Eds. William H. O'Donnell and Douglas N. Archibald. New York: Scribner, 1999.